MUSTANG
A Living Legend

Osprey Colour Series

MUSTANG
A Living Legend

MICHAEL O'LEARY

Published in 1987 by Osprey Publishing Limited
27A Floral Street, London WC2E 9DP
Member company of the George Philip Group

British Library Cataloguing in Publication Data

O' Leary, Michael
    Mustang: a living legend.—(Osprey
    colour series)
    1. Mustang (Figher planes)
    I. Title
    623.74'64   UG1242.F5

ISBN 0-85045-753-X

Editor Dennis Baldry
Designed by David Tarbutt ·
Printed in Hong Kong

Right This is how N6175C looked before
restoration (actually how N6175C #2 began, the
originally-registered aircraft having been written
off many years previously). The wreckage of
N169MD is seen arriving at Unlimited Aircraft
Limited, Chino, California—one of several firms
on the field specializing in Mustang rebuilds.
N169MD had been owned by Dr Burns Byram
who was flying the P-51D when it suffered an
engine failure at night (!). He made a belly-
landing and the pilot and passenger were not
injured, but the Mustang was considered a write-
off (this was in the 1960s when P-51s were not
worth all that much in monetary terms). Byram
purchased another P-51D and also had it
registered N169MD. An experienced pilot, Byram
met his end while ferrying a Mustang back from
Central America during the 1970s. N169MD #1
was stored (fortunately it wasn't scrapped) by
Byram and his estate eventually sold the aircraft
which, along with many other parts, created
N6175C #2. These details drive Mustang
researchers crazy! N6175C is also pictured on
page 60

There can be few aviation enthusiasts who do not appreciate the fine lines and historic exploits of North American Aviation's classic propeller-driven fighter: the Mustang. Originally produced for a British contract and powered with an American Allison engine, the Mustang did not really gain fame until a modified airframe was matched to the Rolls-Royce V-1650 Merlin powerplant. This is not to say that the Allison variants did not do their part during the war—most fought in the low-altitude role until the end of hostilities. But it was the combination of the Mustang with the Merlin that created a long-range escort fighter that could fly into the heart of Germany and Japan, meeting and defeating the best the enemy could offer.

Mustang: A Living Legend concerns itself with Mustangs that are still with us—aircraft that have withstood the difficult test of time to remind us of an age well past. To restore and fly a vintage fighter in the 1980s requires not only skill but a considerable outlay of cash. Once surplused for a few hundred or few thousand dollars, Mustangs are now in demand by collectors and are rapidly approaching the $500,000-mark in value. Around 100 Mustangs currently fly and more restorations are underway as hulks deemed fit for scrap only a few years ago are brought back to life. A few years from now, we will probably be seeing Mustang restoration with as much as 75 per cent of the airframe built from replica parts—such is the demand.

It is difficult to judge just how long Mustangs will continue to fly. There are certainly many obstacles in the way including federal restrictions, the availability of high octane avgas, the aforementioned parts situation (engine parts are particularly critical), and the increasing problem with liability insurance. However long they may fly, we should take full opportunity to enjoy the spectacular sight and sound of these veterans of the past while we still can.

Michael O'Leary is employed as an Editor and Associate Publisher for a large group of aviation magazines. Photography of classic aircraft has always been a hobby and he has had the chance to travel around the world to photograph surviving examples of classic warbirds. The North American Mustang remains his favourite propeller-driven fighter and he is currently working on a project to photograph every flyable Mustang air-to-air.

The photographs for this volume were taken with Nikon and Pentax 35 mm cameras loaded with Kodachrome 25 and 64 film while a Pentax 6×7 was also employed using Ektachrome 64 film. Lenses used varied from 18 mm to 300 mm.

Front cover General Reg Urschler in N5428V paces Pete McManus in his newly-restored *Petie 3rd*; both aircraft are P-51Ds

Back cover Clean machine: a mirror-smooth P-51D illustrates the Mustang's slippery streamlining

Title pages The flight line at San Isidro airbase in the Dominican Republic: two Mustangs of the *Fuerza Aerea Dominicana* (*FAD*) stand alert while the *FAD's* sole flying AT-6 Texan waits in the background

Right One of the rarest airworthy Mustangs is the P-51A-10-NA owned and operated by the Planes of Fame Air Museum at Chino, California. During the early 1950s, museum founder Ed Maloney had his eye on a P-47G and a P-51A used by the Cal-Aero aeronautical training school at Glendale. When the school closed down, Maloney was able to obtain both aircraft and serious restoration work on the P-51D started in the late 1970s. The airplane was in good condition, having been used for hydraulic systems training, and the rebuild proved to be much easier than some of the museum's other restoration projects. Fitted with a freshly overhauled Allison V-1710 engine, the airplane (c/n 99-22354, s/n 43-6251) was registered N4235Y and took to the air again in 1981

Contents

The killer elite

Left Mustang power is well-illustrated in this view of the Hamilton Standard propeller and Rolls-Royce/Packard Merlin installation on N51PT. For its time, the Merlin engine installation and cowling was extremely streamlined, offering a minimum of drag. Note the stainless steel shroud around the exhaust stubs which helped smooth the airflow. However, the shroud was often removed in military service to simplify maintenance. As the Mustang development continued, the number of cowling pieces was reduced—once again to cut maintenance time. The P-51H cowling was considerably updated from the D model

Above The complex personal insignia of John C Meyer's Mustang was faithfully reproduced on Pete McManus' N51PT. Meyer was the top-scoring Mustang ace of the 8th Air Force (flying with the 352nd Fighter Group, 487th Fighter Squadron), achieving 37 kills—24 in the air and 13 on the ground. This close-up shows the amount of detail work lavished on surviving Mustangs by their owners. Highly detailed paint jobs for this type of quality restoration can cost over $20,000

Above John C Meyer named his Mustangs *Petie*, adding a numeral to indicate each different aircraft. The 352nd Fighter Group's Mustangs were identified in the air by having their anti-glare panel and a large portion of the engine cowling painted in a deep, rich blue and aircraft of the 487th Fighter Squadron had their rudders painted the same colour to identify their squadron within the group

Right Pete McManus flies his newly-restored *Petie 3rd* in formation with General Reg Urschler in N5428V. N51PT was built as a P-51D-20-NA at North American Aviation's Inglewood, California, factory (the 'A' in the NA portion of the designation indicates California built while the T in NT means the Mustang was built at NAA's Dallas, Texas, factory). N51PT is construction number (c/n) 122-38604 and United States Army Air Force (USAAF) serial number (s/n) 44-72145. The photograph was taken in June 1985, soon after the rebuild had been completed. N51PT has carried the civil registrations N311G and N6169C

During 1984, Gordon Plaskett of King City, California, restored P-51D-20-NA N5427V (c/n 122-39401, s/n 44-72942) and painted the machine in the markings of John C Meyer's second P-51D, *Petie 2nd*. As can be seen in this view, the markings on Gordon's plane differ from *Petie 3rd*, illustrating revised art work, fewer kills, etc. As with his other Mustang restorations, Plaskett went to a great deal of trouble to ensure accuracy, tracing down crew chiefs and finding the exact shade of the colour of blue used in the 352nd's markings. N5427V had been owned since being surplused in the late 1950s by Robert Fulton (relation of the famous 'Steamboat' Fulton) and had never really been completely civilianized. Fulton used the plane for business transportation and put over 2000 flying hours on the airframe—flying the fighter until he was well into his 70s

The powerful lines of the Mustang are illustrated
in this high-angle view of N5427V during a sortie
from its King City base in December 1984.
During restoration, Plaskett took the Mustang
apart to its basic airframe but did not demate the
wing and fuselage. As with virtually every other
flyable Mustang, the cockpit was modified to take
an additional seat behind the pilot. Out of
accuracy, Gordon decided to leave the instrument
panel in a basically stock condition

P-51D-20-NT N151DM (c/n 111-36533, s/n 44-13250) is painted in the flamboyant markings of Major Pierce McKennon of the 4th Fighter Group. Restored during the mid-1970s for owner Dan Martin, the fighter was built up from Salvadorian Air Force Mustang FAS-411 that had been returned to America. Martin chose McKennon's markings for his restoration because he admired the wild exploits of the 8th AF ace. Basically in stock condition, Dan raced N151DM at Reno several times but, during the 1982 race, the Merlin suffered an engine failure and Dan rode the powerless '51 down to a hard crash landing, the resulting heavy damage keeping the airplane out of the air for two years while rebuilding work was undertaken

After extensive rebuilding, N151DM was put back into the air with its *Ridge Runner III* paint scheme brought back to its full glory. Currently, Martin plans to use the Mustang strictly for pleasure flying and has no intention of returning to Reno for air racing. N151DM serves as a fitting tribute to Pierce McKennon, who, like several other WW2 aces, was killed in a post-war training crash (18 June 1947). P-51B N51PR hangs loose in the background

Above Buckling in. Elmer Ward and a passenger strap into P-51D-25-NA N44727 (c/n 122-39198, s/n 44-72739) for a day's flying at Chino Airport in Southern California. Chino has long been a mecca for surviving Mustangs, several businesses specializing in the restoration of the classic fighter. At one time, the airfield could boast an even two dozen P-51s either flying or under restoration. N44727 was saved from a curious fate by Ascher Ward (no relation) in the early 1970s. The plane was used as a back lot tour attraction at Universal Studios, having last appeared in the motion picture *Battle Hymn*. Through a bit of horse trading, Ward moved the plane by road to nearby Van Nuys Airport where basic restoration work was undertaken—the airframe later being moved to Chino for a complete rebuild by Aero Sport

Left N44727's Merlin belches into life. After restoration by Aero Sport, Ward flew the Mustang for about a year on local flights before selling the airplane to industrialist Elmer Ward. Elmer decided to paint the plane in the colorful markings of Lt Col C H Kinnard and undertook extensive research to insure the insignias and colours were as correct as possible

Above *Man O'War* at its Chino base. Elmer Ward has always been a Mustang buff and he has recently established Pioneer Aero Services at Chino. This long-time company, which Elmer and his sons purchased, has supplied the Mustang needs of foreign air forces and civilian owners for well over two decades. Moving its inventory to Chino, Elmer now has a parts and manufacturing facility as well as a restoration service. The collection was enhanced by the purchase of Lefty Gardner's extensive Mustang inventory, including at least three damaged aircraft that can be brought back to airworthy condition. Ward is also in the process of completing a Grumman F8F-2 Bearcat ground-up restoration

N44727 in flight against a typically smoggy Chino background. Kinnard commanded the 4th Fighter Group from 1 November 1944 through 6 December 1944 while the unit was based at Debden. The 4th had the highest combined air and ground kills of any USAAF fighter unit. From 21 February 1945 to 7 June 1945, Kinnard was in command of the 355th Fighter Group at Steeple Morden, and this unit destroyed more *Luftwaffe* aircraft on the ground than any other USAAF fighter group. N44727 is equipped with the dual Spitfire mirrors favoured by Kinnard

One of the more extensive Mustang restorations is
Pete Regina's P-51B *Shangri-La*. Regina had
always wanted a Mustang but also desired
something more exotic than a bubble-top D. After
reading many books on the subject, he settled on
the B/C variant, the first Rolls-Royce/Packard
variant to go into combat. However, restorable
airframes were virtually extinct and only a couple
of examples survived in museums so it looked like
his first choice of a project would have to give
way to a D or some other type of more available
fighter. This dead-end changed when Pete
discovered an original B model wing—the find
setting him off on a search that would be world-
wide. It would turn out that B/C parts were
almost as difficult to find as restorable airframes

Shangri-La carries the fighting eagle insignia of Debden's 4th Fighter Group. The original *Shangri-La* was written off during a Press demonstration when an over-enthusiastic Gentile flew the airplane into the ground during a high-speed flypast. The P-51B was destroyed and Gentile was assigned back to the States for his mistake. Rumour has it that the wreckage of *Shangri-La* was merely bulldozed into a farmer's pond, its remains still there to this day. N51PR was purchased in 1986 by Mustang collector Joe Kasparoff

Obtaining a corroded P-51D fuselage centre section that had last seen service with the Israeli Air Force, Pete began to restore and modify the unit to B/C configuration—a task of considerable magnitude. A fortuitous discovery was made in the San Francisco area: a large portion of the rear fuselage and tail cone of the last P-51C that had flown in the late 1950s before being written off in a landing accident. This section, coupled with other bits and pieces that were now coming in from around the world, really launched Regina on his project. Careful plaster of paris molds were made from the P-51C on display at the Tallmantz Movieland of the Air in nearby Orange County and missing sections and bulkheads were built from scratch. It was such an extensive project that many people predicted the airplane would be impossible to finish

Late evening sun reflects off N51PR at its Van Nuys base. Regina went to considerable trouble to recreate the colourful markings of high-scoring Mustang ace Don Gentile. Apart from the obvious difference of a built-up canopy and rear structure, the B/C model Mustangs differed in many other ways from the later bubble-topped Ds. There were major differences in the wing and landing gear, four .50 calibre air-cooled Brownings in the B/C's wing as compared to six in the D, cowling differences and a host of other minor changes between the models. B models were built at Inglewood, C models in Dallas

Through constant spare-time work, the P-51B was completed during early 1981 and Pete Regina was able to invite Mustang designer Edgar Schmued to view the aircraft (Pete later gave Schmeud, in his 80s, his first Mustang ride!). The aircraft was painted in the markings of 4th Fighter Group ace Don Gentile before being test flown for the first time by Dave Zeuschel during June 1981. The airplane is seen taxying for its initial hop

DISCIPLINA TRABAJO Y LEALTAD

E-12

Latin American swansong

Left The *Fuerza Aerea Dominicana* was the last air force to operationally fly the Mustang, retiring the remainder of their fleet in 1984. This view shows the main control tower at the *FAD's* main base, San Isidro. This base was developed during the reign of despot Rafael Trujillo when the dictator made the *FAD* the strongest Latin American air arm. Located about twenty miles from the capital, a fine straight road leads directly to the field—the road may have been constructed so that Ramfis Trujillo, appointed to a high *FAD* rank by his father despite the fact he apparently was not a pilot, could set new speed records between the city and base in a variety of exotic sports cars. Trujillo's influence remained long after his just reward—Mustangs remained in operational service for an incredible 36 years. *FAD* motto is Discipline, Work and Loyalty—displayed prominently on the control tower

Main man for the *FAD's* Mustang force. The dynamic *Coronel* Rafael Diaz Bonilla is known to his fellow pilots as *El Diablo Rojo* (The Red Devil) and flew Mustangs from when they were first introduced into the air force. A proponent of *FAD* modernization, Bonilla has survived several crashes in Mustangs. During 1982, Bonilla and 100 fellow pilots flew ten Mustangs, three C-47s, eleven T-34Bs, three AT-6s, ten Cessna T-41s, two Aero Commanders, an MU-2, a Cessna 310 and a Beech Queen Air. Now equipped with Cessna A-37s to replace the Mustangs, the small force still does a creditable job of protecting its area and intercepting some of the numerous drug runners that use the airspace as an entry route to the United States. Bonilla's vast Mustang experience made him the chief P-51 instructor for the *FAD*

Six fully-armed Browning .50 calibre machine guns and a K-14 gunsight indicate that this *FAD* Mustang is ready for any threat. Seen on the ready line at San Isidro, FAD #1912 carries the tactical camouflage that characterized the surviving Mustangs during their last years of service. From the late 1940s on, the *FAD* operated almost 50 Mustangs, most of these eventually being written off in accidents. By the time Trujillo was assassinated on 30 May 1961, the Mustang fleet had become depleted and had taken on a mangey, second-string appearance. *FAD* 1912, a P-51D-20-NA (c/n 122-31910, s/n 44-72051), had seen service with the Royal Swedish Air Force as 26026. Sweden was the main source of *FAD* Mustangs

The Dominican Republic is a poor but proud country—a fact illustrated by the rather crude hand-painted sign at the entrance to San Isidro. Note that the Mustangs are in the 'old' style overall grey scheme that was carried before camouflage was adopted

Above Ready for a training flight. The *FAD's* sole TP-51D, *FAD* 1900, is readied for a flight. Not a true NAA or Temco conversion, this aircraft features a standard canopy while the rear position has a short stick and no true instrument panel—just manifold pressure, rpm, turn and bank, altitude and airspeed gauges mounted in the right and left sides of the cockpit

Right Suited up and ready to go. *El Diablo Rojo* in the cockpit of 1900 before a training flight. At this point in time, July 1982, regular Mustang training was no longer being given—only refresher training. Even so, Bonilla was the last military P-51 instructor in the last military P-51 squadron. With the bubble canopy, full combat gear, and high Dominican temperatures, the cockpit of the Mustang approached the temperature of a greenhouse

Far right *FAD* 1920 maintained on full combat alert at Santiago, a small forward base close to Cuba. Start carts and fire bottles at the ready, two 51s were fully armed and ready for action against a possible Cuban invasion. *FAD* 1920, a P-51D-20-NA (c/n 122-38897, s/n 44-72438), was acquired from Sweden in late 1952, having served with the RSwAF as #26131. Caps over the gun barrels for the six Brownings were supplied from the bottles of a locally-produced rum

Preceding pages *El Diablo Rojo* aloft in *FAD* 1900, the sole dual control P-51 operated by that air force. This view illustrates the underwing rocket rails to advantage. Even though their fighters were virtually antiques, the *FAD* operated the airplanes as military aircraft with no concessions to age—including high-G pullouts from dive bombing and low-level terrain following tactics

Above High over the ocean, two *FAD* Mustangs go about a regular combat patrol. The main enemy of Dominica is Cuba. When a Cuban intelligence vessel ventured into Dominican waters, the Mustangs were scrambled and, when the ship refused to turn back, streams of lead from the Brownings were directed across the vessel's path. Retribution was not long in coming: a force of Cuban MiG-21s beat-up the Dominican coastline. Did the Mustangs rise once more to intercept? No way! 'We went inside and hid until they went away,' recalled one *FAD* pilot. 'What

were we going to do with Mustangs against MiGs?' The leader is the previously described 1912 while his wingman is *FAD* 1916, a P-51D-20-NA (c/n 122-38823, s/n 44-72364, ex-RSwAF 26061). This particular aircraft saw service in WW2 with the 8th Air Force's 353rd FG, 352nd FS, where it carried the name *Upupa Epops* and had ten kills against *Luftwaffe* aircraft

Above This view is indicative of the ancient nature of the *FAD* during the early 1980s. Two Mustangs escort a solitary C-47 Gooney Bird on its way to a paratroop drop. Dominica has always been very pro-American and the officers and men of the *FAD* have had a difficult time understanding American policy in not supplying more modern arms. All their surviving Mustangs were purchased by Brian O'Farrell in 1984 and were offered for sale on the civil market, bringing prices well over $300,000

Left The Dominican national insignia was incorporated into the badge for *Escuadron de Combate*, seen on the vertical tail of *FAD* 1900

Right Maintenance is a never-ending task when you own a Mustang, even though the Mustang required much less maintenance than other American WW2 fighters such as the P-38 and P-47. However, it is a military aircraft—and an old one at that—so the tool box and spare parts supply must never be far away. Ross Grady is seen applying some final touches to his Cavalier Mk 2 Mustang

Flight of four Canadian registered Mustangs over the barren south Texas coastline during October 1979. The first three aircraft carry the fiercesome shark's teeth markings and camouflage of the *Fuerza Aerea Boliviana* while the fourth machine is Jerry Janes' well-known *Cottonmouth*. The first and third aircraft are Cavalier Mk 2s while the second machine, C-GXUO, is a basically stock P-51D. These aircraft were traded for T-33A-Ns during November 1978, giving the Bolivians an armed jet capability and the Canadians lots of fun toys

Perhaps the most flown of the Canadian civil Mustangs is Ross Grady's Cavalier Mk 2 C-GMUS (rebuild completed by Cavalier on 12 February 1968 as s/n 67-22581 for the Military Assistance Program). Grady is a regular attendee of many airshows in the States and in Canada and the rough-finished Mustang is a common sight. This aircraft was originally acquired by Bolivia during the early part of 1968 and disposed of in August 1978 in trade for armed Silver Stars—the Bolivians getting a good solid ten years of service out of the Cavaliers. C-GMUS was *FAB* 523 in Bolivian service. Note that the tip tanks supplied with the Cavalier machines were quickly removed once in service and not restored for civilian use

Preceding pages The Aero Sport storage yard at Chino, California, during 1972: these two derelict Mustangs were purchased by an American collector from the *Corps d'Aviation d'Haiti* when the aircraft were deemed too uneconomical to bring back to flying status. Haiti had a small force of Mustangs, apparently never having more than four operational aircraft with which to counter the Mustangs of neighbouring Dominica. However, Haiti is an even poorer country than the Dominican Republic, especially after the debilitating effects from the excesses of despot 'Papa Doc' Duvalier and his son, the rather porcine 'Baby Doc' Duvalier. These governments, controlled by greed and primitive superstitions, did little to further the Mustang force and the aircraft lapsed into dereliction. As bad as they look (remember this was the early 1970s when disassembled and damaged Mustangs were not worth all that much, a situation that changed considerably in the late 1980s!) both of these aircraft are flying today—although the various

components have been mixed around a bit. These aircraft carried the Haitian serials 916 and 826. Both machines had been liberally splattered with chicken blood by the local ju-ju man in a voodoo ceremony. The yellow bottles in the fuselage constitute the Mustang's oxygen equipment

Above Looking decidedly the worse for wear, this *Fuerza Aerea Salvadorena* Cavalier Mustang Mk 2 rests at Chino Airport on 12 January 1975 after being surplused from *FAS* service in October 1974. N30FF served with the *FAS* as #401. Remanufactured by Cavalier with a completion date of 13 June 1968, the aircraft is now maintained in immaculate condition by Butch Schroeder and extensively flown on the warbird circuit. In common with most Cavalier-delivered Latin American Mustangs, the wingtip fuel tanks were removed to improve handling characteristics. N30FF saw action in the infamous 1969 Soccer War between El Salvador and Honduras which

saw the last piston-engine fighter battles in
history. *Mayor* Soto of Honduras became the last
combat pilot to destroy a Mustang when he shot
down *Capitain* Humberto Varela on 17 July 1969
in an engagement between Soto's F4U-5N Corsair
and Varela's Mustang. A number of US civil
registered Mustangs were sold to Salvador for the
war by American 'preservationists' eager for a
quick buck. Another fighter ripe for preservation
is the California ANG F-102 Delta Dagger (O-
61413) in the background

Boliviana and was photographed at Van Nuys,
California, during March 1982. The Mustang
served with the *Fuerza Aerea Uruguaya* as *FAU*
272 (a P-51D-20-NA), c/n 122-31533, s/n 44-
63807) before being sold to Bolivia

Above With the V-1650-7 Merlin at 61-inches of
manifold pressure and the propeller at 3000 rpm,
Dave Zeuschel has this Mustang flying (but still
riding lightly on the main gear) shortly before
hitting the retract and shoving the gear into the
wells. Zeuschel, the best-known of the Merlin
engine builders, was taking Canadian-registered
C-GXUO on an engine test flight. The aircraft
wears the camouflage of the *Fuerza Aerea*

Overleaf Airborne above a winter wonderland.
Yes, it does snow in Southern California—the
white mountains providing an excellent backdrop
for the camouflaged C-GXUD. FAB-506 has
served with three air forces (USAAF, Uruguay,
and Bolivia), operating in a military role
continuously from 1944 to 1978. Note the
'ancient' ADF football above the rear fuselage.
Dave Zeuschel is seen bringing the Mustang in
close to Pete Regina's P-51B for the photographer

Mustang magnificence

Left The Mustang's powerful lines are well expressed in this near head-on view of Don Davidson's *Double Trouble Two*. Originally built-up by Ray Stutsman, the P-51D-20-NA was painted in the markings of *Double Trouble*. After Davidson purchased the aircraft and flew it for several years, he decided to paint the fighter as *Double Trouble Two*, the second Mustang flown by P-51 ace Lt Col William B Bailey, 352nd Fighter Squadron, 353rd Fighter Group. The carefully applied paint was done by Sky Harbour Refinishers in Goderich, Ontario, Canada

N51EA was purchased by Davidson from Stutsman in April 1982. At that time the restoration had a total of 70 hours and since then Davidson has added 500 more. An airline pilot, he has equipped N51EA with the latest in avionics including a Century III autopilot, an Apollo LORAN-C, and other goodies that enable him to go where other Mustangs fear to tread. Davidson has put well over 60 hours of instrument time on the plane. An added touch of authenticity are the underwing 55 gallon drop tanks, which cause a 10–12 knot loss in speed. This particular aircraft has a wet wing capable of carrying 280 gallons of internal fuel

Above Posed against a placid lake, General Reg Urschler slides in towards the camera ship with P-51D-20-NA N5428V (c/n 122-39723, s/n 44-73264). Urschler, recently retired from the USAF as a Brigadier General, is also a keen warbird buff and regularly flics N5428V to many airshows. He donated the aircraft several years ago to the Confederate Air Force although he retains sponsorship of the vintage fighter. *Gunfighter* was very badly damaged in a landing accident when a sudden gust of wind caught Urschler unprepared, cartwheeling the Mustang and nearly writing off the airplane. Lots of volunteer labour and the infusion of cash and many new airframe parts brought N5428V back to life as *Gunfighter II*, although there is precious little of the original airframe left in the 'new' airplane

Left Urschler's N5428V is equipped with a set of propane-powered 'machine guns', a fairly new development among the warbird set. These fake guns produce a very convincing noise when the trigger is depressed on the control column. The racket is highly appreciated during airshows and adds an element of authenticity to Mustang 'strafing' passes. This view illustrates N5428V's chin air scoop, spinner, and some well-worn Dzus fasteners holding the cowling in place

47

Right Unusual view of Mickey Rupp and his Mustang as they pass under the Beech C-45 Expeditor camera ship. This aircraft is Rupp's fifth Mustang and it has an unusual history. N551MR started out life as P-51D-25-NT (c/n 124-48206, s/n 45-11453) and was surplused in the late 1950s as N5479V. After enjoying a very uneventful civil career, the Mustang was sold in the late 1960s to Aero Sport at Chino, California. Aero Sport gave the plane a brief overhaul for its new owner, *Fuerza Aerea Boliviana*, as FAB-511. The airplane was flown to Bolivia to help beef up their small Mustang contingent on 10 June 1966, along with several other ex-US civil Mustangs. In 1977, the aircraft was one of several traded in for ground attack variants of the Lockheed T-33 Shooting Star. Registered C-GXUP, the airplane rapidly became N59038, N6310T and then N551MR. Mickey had the aircraft completely rebuilt by Darryl Skurich in Ft Collins, Colorado, and painted in this rather creative 'military' scheme. Since this photo was taken, Mickey met up with Brig Gen Chuck Yeager at Oshkosh '86 and Yeager talked Mickey into repainting N551MR in the markings of Bud Anderson, Yeager's WW2 wing leader. The Mustang has subsequently rolled out of the paint shop as Anderson's *Old Crow*

Preceding pages With flaps set at ten degrees south, Bill 'Tiger' Destefani and his Mustang begin to form up with the camera ship. N72FT, a P-51D-30-NA (c/n 122-41035, s/n 44-74494), last served with the Royal Canadian Air Force as #9273 before being sold surplus in the States as N6356T. After passing through several owners, N6356T was fitted with long range tanks and flown to Britain for new owner Charles Masefield. Campaigned at various airshows and meets (it once won the King's Cup race), the Mustang began to fall by the wayside as maintenance became more and more difficult, and the airplane went back to the States in the 1970s, eventually being purchased by Destefani and completely rebuilt. Although appearing fairly stock, N72FT (the FT is for Flying Tiger Farms, Destefani being a farmer by profession) is quite competitive around the Reno pylons where it has been raced several times with varying degrees of success

During the 1950s, 1960s, and for a good part of the 1970s, most surviving Mustangs were painted in a variety of civil colour schemes—military-style markings as yet had little or no impact. Mustang owner Gary McCann, who divides his time between his native Canada and a more hospitable Florida, maintains his P-51D-20-NA (c/n 122-31615, s/n 44-63889) in black and white civilian colours. The aircraft carries the scheme designed by David Lindsay of Cavalier Aircraft in the late 1950s, a style which was applied to most of the Mustangs that facility rebuilt or modified and a style which did little to improve or enhance the P-51's looks. This aircraft was originally-registered N7710C when surplused in the States, and when McCann obtained the aircraft he originally had the Mustang registered CF-FUK—markings which did not take the Canadian officials overly long to cancel!

Sometimes Mustangs are brought back to life through individual perseverance and N65206 is such an example. Over a period of several years, owner John Marlin worked diligently to rebuild and repair the airframe of P-51D-30-NΛ (c/n 122-40998, s/n 44-74458), heavily damaged during the early 1960s following a forced landing in a muddy field. The Mustang, at that time registered N9145R, flipped over on its back after touch down. Fortunately, the airplane was not scrapped and it was shuttled through several owners before being purchased by Marlin, who singlehandedly restored it to flying condition. N65206's last military service was with the RCAF as #9226. The Mustang is painted in the scheme of a P-51B converted to test the new bubble canopy developed by North American

Immaculately painted P-51D N51WB is owned by Bill Clark of State College, Pennsylvania. As with some Mustangs, the history of this particular aircraft is somewhat shadowy. 'It was returned to the United States from Salvador where it had been smuggled in for the 1969 war between that country and Honduras. The true identity of the aircraft was eradicated but, with the help of Mustang International, we think the serial is 44-74960,' stated Clark

Right Continuing on N51WB's history, Clark commented, 'If that is indeed the serial, then the Mustang was delivered to the USAAF in 1945 and served with the 182nd Fighter Bomber Squadron and other Stateside units. It was surplused in February 1958. After being returned to the States, the Mustang was registered as N34FF and sold to Scott Smith. I was the next owner.' Bill Clark began WW2 as a liaison pilot, and ended up as a crew chief on B-25s. Keeping the vintage fighter in perfect flying trim is a costly task. 'I had the four fuselage longerons replaced by LyCon Aviation and that was a major, and expensive, piece of work,' recalls Clark. 'They removed one longeron at a time and then added the replacement unit. This way the fuselage stayed in rig and the airplane now flies just the same as it did before the longeron replacement'

Above The paint scheme on Bill Clark's Mustang came about in an interesting manner. 'One of the residents of my hometown flew with the 339th Fighter Group and told me about a pilot with the same name as mine. Sure enough, after checking the facts, I found Colonel Bill Clark and got in touch with him in Ft Myers, Florida, and he kindly provided me with some rare colour photos of his P-51D, named *HAPPY IV*. I liked the scheme and had Tom Crevasse in Greenwood, Mississippi, do the painting. I took a couple of liberties with Clark's scheme, replacing several things I didn't like. The rudder was originally a nasty green colour so I changed that. The name *Dottie* was on the canopy frame but, in the original photo, it looked more like *Dolly* because of the style the British painter employed. Clark told me they were very lax about paint schemes. He said one day he went to the field for a mission and found the green rudder replaced by a blue unit with white stars. Apparently his crew chief did not care for the colour, either'

Right *Worry Bird* is a lovely Mustang restoration (and EAA Oshkosh warbird grand champion award-winner) built-up and restored by Jack Rose of Spangle, Washington. N51DF is a P-51D-20-NA (c/n 122-39746, s/n 44-73287) and was formerly N5445V. Rebuilt over a period of several years, Rose had the airframe highly polished and finished in the markings of the 503rd Fighter Squadron, 339th Fighter Group. Unfortunately, while landing at Cannon Airport, Reno, Nevada, to visit the 1986 Reno Air Races, Jack had one landing gear hang up—resulting in a 'one up, one down' landing with corresponding damage. Fortunately, the airplane received only minor injuries

P-51D-20-NA N5460V (c/n 122-38651, s/n 44-72192) is owned and operated by California Warbirds—a unique club-like organization that sells shares in its Mustang. For a certain amount of money, a member can purchase a share and then fly the P-51 for a fixed per hour cost, part of the money going into a fund for maintenance, engine replacement, etc. A similar club in Los Angeles operated two Mustangs, both of which were destroyed in fatal accidents

N5460V taxies in at the 1981 Madera, California, Gathering of Warbirds airshow (an event that has, on several occasions, had over two dozen Mustangs on display). *Straw Boss 2* is finished in the markings of the 328th Fighter Squadron, 352nd Fighter Group

Left Over the top. Skip Holm rolls P-51D N6175C up and over the camera ship with a half moon hanging in the background. This particular aircraft was assembled from the parts of several other Mustangs damaged in accidents. N6175C is now regularly raced at Reno as #39, *The Healer*. Mustangs are of such high value that any part left over from an accident quickly finds its way into a restoration. Several firms are currently manufacturing brand-new P-51 components such as air scoops, fairings, etc—all built to conform exactly with the original

Above After WW2, the P-51D and P-51H formed the backbone for the majority of USAF Air National Guard fighter squadrons. It is appropriate that several restored Mustangs have now been finished in ANG markings—including N51HR. This P-51D-20-NA (c/n 122-31268, s/n 44-63542, ex-N5450V) is painted in Nevada ANG markings, 'The High Rollers', which is appropriate since owner Ted Contri keeps his Mustang at Reno Cannon Airport, home of the Nevada ANG Phantoms

Towards the end of WW2, North American redesigned a P-51D fuselage to accommodate two pilots and a full set of dual controls. This modification was made to reduce training accidents and expedite type-conversion. However, since the war was virtually over, the TP (later TF) Mustang was never more than a very limited production item. For the Korean War, Temco Aircraft acquired the rights for the TF and produced another limited run of two-seaters. Cavalier Aircraft Corporation also produced their own version of the TF in the 1960s and 1970s for supply to foreign governments. P-51D-20-NA (c/n 122-39917, s/n 44-73458, ex-N36FF, FAS 404, N554T, N6347T, RCAF 9294) N4151D was purchased by the government of El Salvador and used a Cavalier conversion kit to produce a dual-control TF. Damaged in service, the remains were purchased and rebuilt by Gordon Plaskett. The Mustang eventually passed into the hands of the Whittington brothers who added their usual custom touches such as a one-piece windshield and red leather interior. This Mustang served with three different air forces

Dennis Bradley, president of the Canadian Warplane Heritage, displays the lines of the CWH's 'new' Mustang, C-FBAU. This airplane carries the same registration as the CWH's first Mustang which was completely destroyed by fire following engine failure and an emergency landing. C-FBAU is a P-51D-25-NA (c/n 122-39281, s/n 44-72826) which had been owned by Tom Watson in the States as N6344T before sale to the CWH. This particular aircraft had actually served with the Royal Canadian Air Force as #9563

Left Business end of C-FBAU #2: all P-51Ds were equipped with six .50 calibre air-cooled Browning machine guns. The civilian machines, of course, had the armament removed before being sold, but the majority of civil owners during the late 1950s and 1960s went a step further and removed the ports, thus giving a flush leading edge. Most Mustangs flying today have had the gun ports put back in place

Above Mickey Rupp in N551MR flies left wing on Connie and Ed Bowlin in N551CB, a P-51D-25-NT (c/n 124-48134, s/n 45-11381, ex-C-GXLR, N5471V). Well-known as *The Flying Undertaker*, the Mustang was virtually written off after a landing accident. The wreck was purchased by Ritchie Rasmussen in Canada and rebuilt back to flying status. After several years, Ritchie sold the Mustang to Ed and Connie, both professional pilots for Delta Airlines. They painted the fighter in the WW2 markings of Captain Chuck Yeager and take turns flying the impeccably maintained classic to airshows across America

Right Same markings, different Mustang. When a Mustang was needed for a battery company's television commercial featuring retired Brig Gen Chuck Yeager, the well-known P-51D-30-NT from The Air Museum, Chino, California, was drafted into portraying Yeager's WW2 mount. Previously named *Spam Can*, N5441V (c/n 124-48335, s/n 45-11582) was painted up in Yeager's colours and used in the commercial. Rick Bricket is seen posing the fighter during May 1983

Preceding pages Jimmie Hunt brings N5551D into formation with the camera ship. P-51D-20-NA (c/n 122-40223, s/n 44-73683) was previously registered N12064 and had last served with the *Fuerza Aerea de la Guardia Nacional de Nicaragua* before being sold with other surviving *FAN* Mustangs to the States in the early 1960s

D model in B colours. Owner Jim Beasley was particularly taken with the WW2 colours and markings of a P-51B named *Bald Eagle*. Accordingly, after N51JB had been restored by Unlimited Aircraft Limited, the fighter was finished in *Bald Eagle's* attractive markings. The Mustang carries the codes of the 374th Fighter Squadron, 361st Fighter Group

N51JB began life at Inglewood as a P-51D-25-NA (c/n 122-39488, s/n 44-73079, ex-N7999A). As with many of the Mustangs flying today, there is some doubt about the aircraft's actual identity. Since photographs exist of a very wrecked N7999A, it is possible that the aircraft was rebuilt. If the identity is correct, then N51JB last served operationally with the *Fuerza Aerea de la Guardia Nacional de Nicaragua* as GN-122. Before being surplused from the States, the Mustang last served with the Ohio Air National Guard's 112th Fighter Squadron. It was one of a group of Nicaraguan Mustangs returned to the United States in 1963

It is a sobering thought to realize that after this formation photograph was taken during June 1983, one of them was completely destroyed and another damaged in a belly landing. The lead Mustang, the all-black N5449V flown by Earl Ketchen, was demolished after failing to recover from an acrobatic manoeuvre – killing Ketchen and his passenger. The middle Mustang, N63810, was damaged afterwards in a gear-up landing. Fortunately, the last Mustang, N55JL, is happily active as both a sport plane and air racer

Earl Ketchen in N5449V over a Texas landscape. This aircraft was used as both an Unlimited air racer and as a sport plane. For racing, the outer wing panels would be removed and racing tips added. Other race modifications built into the aircraft include the odd airflow strakes behind the radiator scoop and the small wing fences between the ailerons and flaps

One of the rarest of Mustangs is Mike Coutches'
P-51H—the last of the flying 'lightweight'
Mustangs. Coutches assembled the aircraft from a
left over NACA airframe along with other various
bits and pieces to create a superb example of the
last of the production Mustangs. Built in fairly
large numbers (555), the H was never destined to
see combat or foreign service

N551H is equipped with non-standard underwing
long-range tanks. The H was the result of a severe
weight reduction programme to create a faster-
climbing, more manoeuvrable fighter. According
to some pilots, it was a waste of effort. 'It was a
pig,' recalls Brig Gen Chuck Yeager. 'It wasn't as
good as the D model and it was an extremely
tiring aircraft to fly.' The H's armament was
reduced to four .50 calibre Browning machine
guns

N551H is just one of Coutches' stable of warbirds, which includes other Mustangs, a Bearcat, and a Hellcat. The H model remains one of his favourites and it is maintained in excellent condition. The larger, more streamlined H canopy is apparent in this view. When the Korean War started, Hs were available in some numbers but they did not have the load carrying capability of the D model or the Corsair, and were not pressed into service

As we come towards the end of the 1980s, a new trend in warbird ownership is becoming more and more evident. Well-heeled warbird owners with the bucks to buy more aircraft are doing just that. One of the prime examples is John Macguire of Texas who is seen roaring along in P-51D-25-NT (c/n 124-44706, s/n 44-84850) N87JB which he had restored from an Indonesian Air Force airframe that was returned to the States in the late 1970s

Overleaf N87JB is just one of several ex-Indonesian Mustangs owned by John MacGuire of El Paso. The other aircraft are under restoration to join his fleet of warbirds, which include an F-86 Sabre and a TF-51D in flying trim

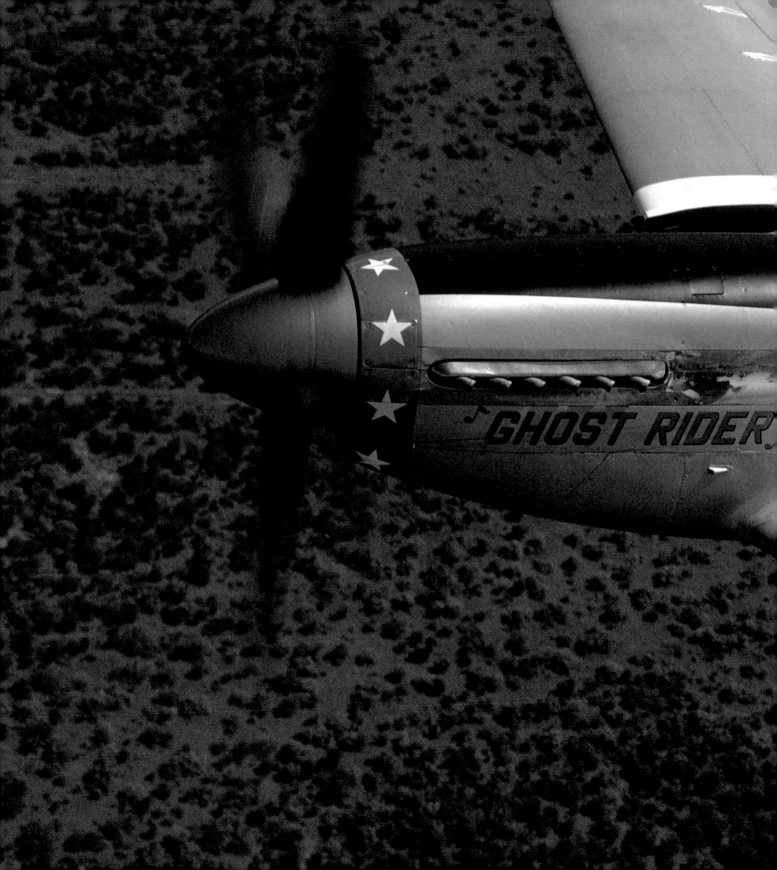

This Mustang virtually changes its colours each year. N55JL is owned and raced by Jimmie Leeward and, almost every year, sports a new set of markings or trim. At Reno '86, Leeward—who also owns the highly-modified P-51D N79111—was able to field the first father/son Unlimited racing team. Jimmie flew N79111 while Dirk Leeward took over the flying duties of clipped-wing N55JL and put in a creditable performance. N55JL is a P-51D-25-NT (c/n 124-44471, s/n 44-84615, ex-N9LT, N7099V) and last saw active service with the Israeli Air Force before being exported to California during the 1960s where it sat abandoned in a crate for several years

Bob Byrne's *Rascal* is an ex-Royal Canadian Air
Force Mustang (RCAF 9270) which had
previously seen service with the USAAF as s/n
44-74774

Ritchie Rasmussen in C-GXLR, *The Flying Undertaker*, a Mustang which he painstakingly rebuilt from a badly damaged wreck. Ritchie purchased the remains of N5471V and spent a couple of years breathing life back into the airframe. Ritchie eventually sold the plane to Ed and Connie Bowlin and it is illustrated elsewhere in this volume. *Undertaker* carries the markings of Major William Shomo who, before becoming a fighter pilot, was an undertaker by profession. Shomo shot down seven Japanese aircraft in one day—gaining the Medal of Honor for his exploit

The late, lamented C-FBAU #1 seen in flight over Titusville, Florida, in company with Howard Pardue and his Grumman XF8F-1 Bearcat. As related elsewhere in this issue, C-FBAU was completely destroyed in a fire which resulted from a forced landing after engine failure. S/n 44-73140 was operated by the Canadian Warplane Heritage and flown by Dennis Bradley. About the only items left after the accident were the wingtips

Top left 'Old Red Nose' is the affectionate name given to the Mustang owned and operated by the Confederate Air Force. One of the first aircraft in the CAF's now vast fleet, this Mustang has served faithfully for over two decades of civil operations. CAF members interested in the Mustang help sponsor the aircraft. This means they pay a certain fee that is set aside for aircraft maintenance and repair. In turn, after they are given a thorough checkout, they are allowed to fly it. N10601 is a P-51D-20-NA (c/n 122-40383, s/n 44-73843, ex-RCAF #9271) and can usually be found at its Harlingen, Texas, home base. Old Red Nose is seen high over Houston during September 1986's Wings Over Houston airshow

Left A Mustang with an interesting history: Robb Satterfield's N7722C served with the USAF during WW2 and Korea then, as a civilian

aircraft, went on to serve as an aerial platform for weapons developed for the Vietnam conflict. *Miss Torque* (P-51D-20-NA, c/n 122-39879, s/n 44-73420) has received a brilliant polish for its aluminum skin. Veteran USAF fighter pilot Satterfield often uses the aircraft for a professional aerobatic routine at airshows

Above Down but not out. A bit bent and dusty, P-51D-30-NA N100D (c/n 122-41463, s/n 44-74923, ex-N132, N5438V) is seen after a classic belly landing following engine failure at the September 1983 edition of the Reno National Air Races. The Mustang, owned by John Sandberg, and flown by Chuck Hall, passed home pylon before the Merlin came to pieces and caused this firm arrival on a chunk of Reno desert. N100D was flying a few months later courtesy of Steve Hinton's Fighter Rebuilders

Preceding pages Wolfpack on the prowl. The 1986 Canadian Warplane Heritage airshow at Hamilton, Ontario, Canada, saw sixteen pristine P-51Ds on the flight line. This view shows four of the aircraft in flight. Led by Pete McManus in N51PT, the rest of the flight comprises Hess Bomberger in N6320T, Don Davidson in N51EA, and Bill Clark's N51WB

Above Another veteran rebuilt to beautiful flying condition. This Australian-built Commonwealth Aircraft Corporation CA17 Mk 20 Mustang had served with the Royal Australian Air Force as A68-39 before being surplused as VH-BOY. In its civilian career, VH-BOY led a long and hard life as a target tug. Many modifications were incorporated for the towing mission and the airplane was in less than ideal shape when it arrived at Bill Destefani's restoration shop at Shafter, California. But Bill's talented crew brought 'BOY back to life and, now registered as N551D, the Mustang is owned and flown by Jack Erikson in Oregon

With its V-1650-7 Merlin singing its distinctive
song, Fred Sebby pilots N3278D above the Chino,
California, smog. Painted in attractive Royal Air
Force colours, this P-51D has been raced several
times at Reno—its basic stock configuration
limiting the fighter to the Bronze event (reserved
for the stock, or slower Unlimiteds)

Classic iron in formation: Lloyd Hamilton flies right wing with his Sea Fury as Art Vance slots his Mustang into formation with the camera aircraft. Vance's Mustang carries the coding of the 364th FS, 347th FG while Art's choice of the name *Million Dollar Baby* is particularly appropriate. At the time of writing, the average price for a restored P-51D is between $300 and $400,000 and is constantly rising with little sign of slowing down. N64824 is a Commonwealth Aircraft Corporation CA18 Mk 23 Mustang (c/n 1500) that served with the Royal Australian Air Force as A68-175

Down and dirty: Bill Hane shows what a Mustang looks like with gear and flaps down. N151X carries the name *Ho! Hun* and is a P-51D-30-NT (c/n 124-48381, s/n 45-11628, ex-N5446V) used by Hane for airshow flying where he puts on a superior aerobatic act with the Mustang

The Enforcer

Left The saga of the Mustang as a combat aircraft came full circle with the Piper PA-48 Enforcer. Brainchild of David Lindsay (founder of Cavalier Aircraft and top proponent of the Mustang design), the Enforcer was conceived by Lindsay as a logical follow-on to the classic North American design. Lindsay originally had two Enforcers built in the early 1970s, one being lost in a crash. By using his considerable influence in Congress during the early 1980s, Lindsay had a Bill passed that called for the construction of two new Enforcers (with considerable improvements) to possibly fulfill a USAF requirement for a replacement for the ground attack A-10 'Warthog'. Test pilot David Lawrence is seen with the two PA-48 Enforcers at Edwards AFB during August 1984

Above For the tank-busting role, the PA-48 was designed to carry massive 30 mm cannon pods under the wings—a weapon essential to the anti-tank mission. However, these huge pods would have degraded Enforcer performance to a considerable extent. David Lawrence and other Piper personnel completed 208 sorties with the Enforcer from the Piper facility at Lakeland, Florida, sixty sorties involving weapon compatibility testing from Eglin AFB, and sixty-nine out of a possible ninety-five sorties from Edwards AFB, where operational testing was carried out. When the time came for USAF test pilots to fly the Enforcer, the USAF refused and no Air Force pilot flew the PA-48

Unusual view of N481PE, the first PA-48, being flown by David Lawrence. The morning sun at high altitude shows the coarse, radar-absorbent nature of the European One-style camouflage scheme. One of Lawrence's main complaints about poor performance of the prototypes was Piper's use of extremely 'fat' underwing pylons (ten in all) which reduced airspeed considerably. Production Enforcers would have been equipped with much slimmer pylons

Above Down and dirty. High above the clouds, David Lawrence drops the gear on PA-48 #1 to show the aircraft's definite Mustang influence. Tyres and wheels came off a Grumman Gulfstream and the slim, high pressure units made testing from soft surfaces a washout. From Day One, the USAF bitterly fought the manufacture of the Enforcer—not wanting anything to do with propeller-driven aircraft that had tailwheels, even if they made sense in a combat situation. The ten underwing pylons on the Enforcer would have been capable of carrying a wide variety of contemporary USAF ground attack weapons

Overleaf Under an $11,000,000 contract, Piper Aircraft (a company not exactly known for building warplanes) began construction of the two PA-48 prototypes. The production PA-48 was to be an all-new aircraft but, unfortunately, three P-51Ds 'died' during the construction of the two Enforcers. David Lawrence is seen showing off his considerable formation skills with the second Enforcer, N482PE. Powered by a YT55-L-9A Lycoming turboprop of 2445 shaft horsepower, the Enforcer was capable of a top speed of 318 knots. (Lawrence was of the opinion that the airframes needed a considerable aerodynamic clean-up, again a facet of Piper's unfamiliarity with combat aircraft)

Vizor down to protect his eyes against a brilliant
California sun, David Lawrence brings N481PE in
for a low-angle view. The lines running through
the canopy are explosive cord that would shatter
the Plexiglass in case of ejection. As can be seen,
the canopy is much larger than the standard P-
51D unit. This view also shows how the huge
exhaust for the Lycoming turboprop is masked by
the wing, thus reducing the infrared signature.
Production Enforcers would have been powered
with an uprated T55L capable of pumping out
3000 shp for a top speed of 350 knots with a war
load. The two prototypes were turning cut-down
Douglas Skyraider propellers

The two Enforcers sit on the ramp at Edwards
AFB. The USAF attitude towards the project was
almost hostile. USAF test pilots would probably
have had their hands full with the machines since
hardly any of them had the relevant experience.
The huge exhausts were carefully canted to
counter any torque from the Skyraider propeller.
Both Enforcers were equipped with Stencel
extraction seats. Testing revealed that the canopy
was much too large and it would have been
smaller on production machines

Top left With the Enforcer programme pretty well written-off, it can be safely assumed that the long service life of the Mustang has finally come to an end—a record unsurpassed by any propeller-driven fighter. And for the two surviving PA-48s? Who knows—they may well join their brothers on the civilian warbird circuit!

Left Officials from several foreign air forces were interested in the Enforcer programme but lack of USAF interest precluded the possibility of any orders. Extensive computer work proved that the Enforcer probably would have performed effectively in a forward airfield role against enemy armour. However, the USAF felt that the A-10A performed the same mission and was already in service. It is interesting to note that the USAF is currently interested in finding an A-10A replacement, feeling that the aircraft may be too vulnerable and ineffective in the vital NATO environment

Above During August 1984, David Lawrence had the sad task of ferrying both PA-48s from Edwards AFB to Davis-Monthan AFB—the 'bone yard' for the military's cast-off aircraft. Both Enforcers had their systems inhibited and any openings were sealed with a spray-on preservative to await an uncertain future. One Enforcer was loaned to the nearby Pima County Air Museum where it sits baking in the Arizona sun

Mustang round up

Above Each P-51D bubble canopy is a bit different because the units are individually free blown. Most replacement items for Mustangs have risen rapidly in value over the last few years, sometimes by as much as 1000 per cent (yes, *one thousand!*)

Left Airpower at its best. Sixteen beautifully restored P-51Ds are seen on the flight line at the Canadian Warplane Heritage's June 1986 airshow. Such large numbers of the famous fighter are not uncommon. There are just over 100 flying examples of the Mustang in the United States and that number is slowly increasing as airframes are returned from other countries for restoration

Colours of combat. As the war progressed, the Mustang shed its olive drab and neutral grey camouflage scheme in favour of bare metal with bright unit markings. As the value of the Mustang has increased, most owners have taken considerable care to insure their machines are painted in the accurate markings of combat fighters

Right The sun gleams off the burnished aluminum skin of Mustang N286JB, the Rolls-Royce emblem prominent in this close-up view. After the conclusion of WW2, Rolls-Royce pulled its Merlin license from Packard—forcing the majority of the new F-82 Twin Mustangs to be engined with Allison V-1710s. The story had come full circle since the first Mustang, the NA-73X, was fitted with the Allison powerplant

A typical civilian Mustang of the early 1970s. Photographed during March 1974, N634OT wears a not unattractive bright red and white colour scheme. At this point in time, only a few Mustang owners were beginning to realize the historical significance of their machines and painting them in authentic colours. N634OT would have a long way to go before wearing a combat uniform once again

It's hard to believe this is N634OT, but it's the same airplane with new colours. After our first photo was taken, '4OT had a career as an Unlimited racer and then as a sport plane before being sold to aircraft collector Stephen Grey in Britain. At Oakland, California, Mike Bogue rigged '4OT with huge underwing tanks and the aircraft was flown to Britain by well-known Mustang racing pilot John Crocker. On arrival

'4OT was given this attractive scheme (362nd Fighter Squadron, 357th Fighter Group) and hit the airshow circuit with an enthusiastic Grey. The Mustang (a P-51D-20-NA, c/n 122-39608, s/n 44-73149, ex-RCAF # 9568) was the start of his extensive Duxford-based warbird collection and he is seen in formation with his Republic Thunderbolt, flown by Steve Hinton, over Duxford

Engine run *numero uno*: anyone that's been around Mustangs for any length of time knows that considerable effort is expended on engine runs—making sure the thing is running correctly, checking oil pressure and temp's, etc. N651D is seen preparing for engine start at Van Nuys, California, on 8 July 1972 (it didn't happen, the magnetos were incorrectly installed). As can be seen, the aircraft was in the process of a minor rebuild for a new owner. Unfortunately, the aircraft did not survive the decade, plunging to earth with P-51D CF-USA after the two Mustangs flew into a thunderstorm while returning from an airshow

Engine run *numero due*: searching for a spot of magneto trouble, Don Davidson exercises the V-1650 of his *Double Trouble*, N51EA, while mechanics look on. Don has lavished lots of care on his P-51D and photographs of the repainted *Double Trouble Two* can be found elsewhere in this volume

Engine run *numero tre*: Merlin builder Dave Zeuschel cranks over the Merlin in CAC Mustang Mk 23 N4674V (c/n 1523, A68-198) at Chino, California, during March 1975 in front of the fabled Aero Sport hangar (careful scanning of the original photo shows at least twelve Mustangs receiving maintenance inside the hangar). This Australian-built Mustang later became N286JB which is pictured on the right. Australian constructed Mustangs made extensive use of anodized aluminum and these show up on the airframe as the darker panels. Zeuschel is concerned over the dwindling supply of Merlin parts and is of the opinion that some assemblies will have to be put back into limited production if Mustangs are to continue flying

The classic Merlin exhaust pattern is clearly
etched on the polished sides of N286JB. An
extremely clean running engine, the Merlin has
gained a well-deserved reputation for reliability
and ruggedness

Cowlings off, a Packard V-1650-7 Merlin nestles in the motor mount of a P-51D. Although the rocker covers have been emblazoned with Rolls-Royce, the engine is actually Packard-built, as are most of the Merlins flying in American Mustangs. Although basically similar, Packard did change quite a few items on the V-12 to suit American production techniques

Cowlings start coming off and its time for the
never-ending maintenance and care that is
required to keep these vintage fighters airworthy.
N51AB is seen receiving some work prior to flying
at the annual Confederate Air Force show in
Harlingen, Texas. This particular aircraft is a
Commonwealth Aircraft Corporation CA18 Mk 21
(c/n 1425) and flew with the RAAF as A68-100.
After being sold from military service, the
Mustang became VH-BOW before being imported
to the States for new owner Robby Jones

During the late 1970s, the island nation of Indonesia became a fertile hunting ground for old Mustangs. Indonesia had operated many Mustangs over the years and, in the 1970s, had received an infusion of Cavalier rebuilt aircraft as part of a US military aid programme. However, the aircraft did not last long before being put up for disposal. Most of the Mustangs and their parts inventory were purchased by Steve Johnson. Johnson took the pick of the litter and then began selling off the disassembled Mustangs as kits. Al Letcher of Mojave, California, purchased one of the kits and the result is seen after restoration. P-51D-25-NA (c/n 122-39236, s/n 44-72777, TNI-AU:F-344) N8064V was painted in Pacific Theatre markings and named *Singapore Sally*. Letcher has since sold it to Steve Seghetti who has re-registered the machine as N151D

Late afternoon sun on 15 January 1974 highlights
Steve Schulke as he taxies N2251D to the runway.
This aircraft was aerobatic pilot Bob Hoover's
famous 'Yellow Bird' before being grounded by an
accident caused by filling the fuselage oxygen
battles until they burst. The fuselage was split
open and its back broken. The remains of
N2251D were combined with the wreck of another
civil Mustang to create the 'new' N2251D.
Schulke was later killed in a T-34 accident and
the Mustang passed to a new owner

The only flying A-36 Mustang dive bomber, A-36A-1-NA N251A (c/n 97-15949, s/n 42-83731) was purchased as a hulk and rebuilt by Dick Martin for owner Tom Friedkin at Palomar, California. Only 500 A-36s were built and they featured dive brakes in the wing and pylons for bombs under the wing. Powered by the Allison V-1710, the A-36s were extremely effective in their assigned task and fought with the USAAF all through the war, by the end of which there were few surviving A-36s. A non-flying example of the A-36 is on display at the USAF Museum

A Mustang rebuilder's dream project: this Philippine Air Force P-51D has seen better days but it certainly could be put back into the air—all it takes is work and money. Parked at a small PAF display at Manila Airport, the Mustang has had many of its more easily removed bits and pieces taken and replaced by definately non-airworthy units (note the fairings, landing gear doors, cowling, etc). Fortunately, these items were utilized to help restore a Mustang to airworthy status

All the way from Taihiti (by boat, not air). F-AZAG is a French-registered Cavalier-modified Mustang (note taller vertical tail) that was operated for several years by a French owner in Taihiti. Returned to the States, the aircraft was refurbished at Aero Sport to stock configuration and given a WW2 military paint scheme. The P-51D-20-NA (c/n 122-39665, s/n 44-73206, ex-N7724C) is now registered N3751D. Cavalier was responsible for converting many Mustangs into 'executive' configuration during the 1960s and these mods included airframe and avionic updates, taller vertical tail and, quite often, large tip tanks. Cavalier was also responsible for rebuilding many of the Latin American air forces' Mustangs. Owner David Lindsay was directly responsible for saving many Mustangs and establishing the type as the most numerous of all surviving WW2 fighters

Most Mustangs flying today are equipped with the
latest avionics, several aircraft being fully
equipped for all-weather operation. The panel of
C-GJCJ is seen when the Canadian-registered
aircraft was owned by Jerry Janes

Power check. Gary McCann guns the Merlin in C-FFUZ to discover the cause of an RPM drop. Merlins were once plentiful but the supply of spare engines has really dried up (prices escalating at the same time) due to intensive use of the engine in occupations such as power-boat racing— a sport that has gobbled up hundreds of Merlins. Most Mustangs are equipped with V-1650-7 V-12s which develop a maximum (stock) horsepower rating of 1450 hp at 3000 rpm and 61-inches of manifold pressure

Like a shark fin, the vertical tail of Gary
McCann's C-FFUZ is seen protruding from a
line-up of airshow warbirds

Few items of decoration add a more fearsome note to a fighter plane's snout than a well-executed set of shark (or tiger) teeth. This deadly grin is recorded on Ross Grady's Cavalier Mk 2 Mustang

Old West gunman illustrates the side of Reg
Urschler's *Gunfighter II*. This aircraft has had the
stainless steel shrouds removed from around the
exhaust stacks

Warbird owner Bob Byrne likes Mustangs—and he likes yellow and red. Bob's D model *Rascal* is a regular visitor to airshows across the United States

Sleekly elegant cowl of the P-51D owned by Ed
and Connie Bowlin. Most current restorations
make use of a silver or aluminum paint instead of
going with bare metal (Ds were delivered from the
factory in a bare metal finish but an aluminum
paint was used on most of the wing in order to
maintain the laminar flow aerodynamics). The use
of paint makes the exterior surface easier to
maintain while helping cover the various signs of
usage accumulated over 40 years

Ain't Misbehavin was the name of a popular wartime song so it is fitting that it's carried on the side of P-51D-20-NA N988C (c/n 122-40549, s/n 44-74009, ex-N6323T, RCAF #9275) owned by Bob Ferguson

Here's another view of N988C taken two years
earlier (June 1984) when the Mustang had a red
and silver scheme rather than the new blue and
white. As can be seen, *Ain't Misbehavin* carries a
large Rolls-Royce emblem on the side of the
cowling. Some owners have had their Mustangs
for over 20 years and during that time it is not
uncommon for paint schemes to change several
times

Above Exhaust plugs firmly in place, P-51D-20-NA N576GF (c/n 122-39438, s/n 44-73029) stands down after a day of airshow flying. Flown by Korean War MiG-ace Bob Love, the right side of the aircraft carries the markings and insignia of partner Cliff Jolley

Left Pirate's flag adorns the side of N576GF. This particular aircraft had a fair racing career as a modified Unlimited before being rebuilt back into relatively stock condition

Overleaf Mustang rampant. During the 1980s, the P-51 Mustang has enjoyed unprecedented popularity as an airshow performer. However, many pilots question just how long these old warhorses can continue flying. Problems such as the availability of spares (especially for the engine), decreasing supplies of avgas, and the rapidly increasing spectre of liability insurance may well put the Mustang back in the barn. Until that time, this classic warplane should be appreciated as a fabulous piece of living history